This
Cruise Trip Journal
Belongs To

....

....

....

Cruise Month Planner

SUN	MON	TUE	WED	THU	FRI	SAT

NOTES

....
....
....
....

Before We Go

Our Cruise Ship

....

Dates of Travel

....

Ports We Will Visit

....
....
....
....
....
....
....
....

About Me

My age ....

I like to ....
....
....
....
....

Favorite Movies

....
....
....

Favorite Movie Characters

....
....
....

NOTES

....
....
....
....

Packing Checklist

 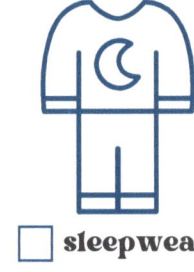  

☐ underwear ☐ sleepwear ☐ swimwear ☐ socks

☐ jeans ☐ shirt ☐ dress ☐ hoodie

 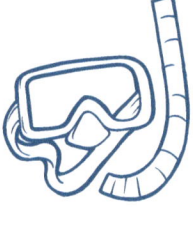  

☐ goggles ☐ snorkel ☐ cap / hat ☐ sunglasses

☐ sneakers ☐ hiking boots ☐ flipflops / sandals

Packing Checklist

Others:

- [ ] ....
- [ ] ....
- [ ] ....
- [ ] ....
- [ ] ....
- [ ] ....
- [ ] ....
- [ ] ....
- [ ] ....
- [ ] ....
- [ ] ....
- [ ] ....
- [ ] ....
- [ ] ....

My State Room

Room Number

Type of Cabin
....

Cabin Steward
....

Favorite Towel Animal
....

Ship Director
....

My Stateroom is really close to
....
....
....

My Stateroom is really far from
....
....
....

What I like about the stateroom
....
....
....
....
....
....

Embarkation Day

Today's Date

....

First impressions of the ship

....
....
....
....
....

Sail Away Party - What did I see? What did I do?

....
....
....
....
....

What am I most excited about doing this trip?

....
....
....
....
....
....
....

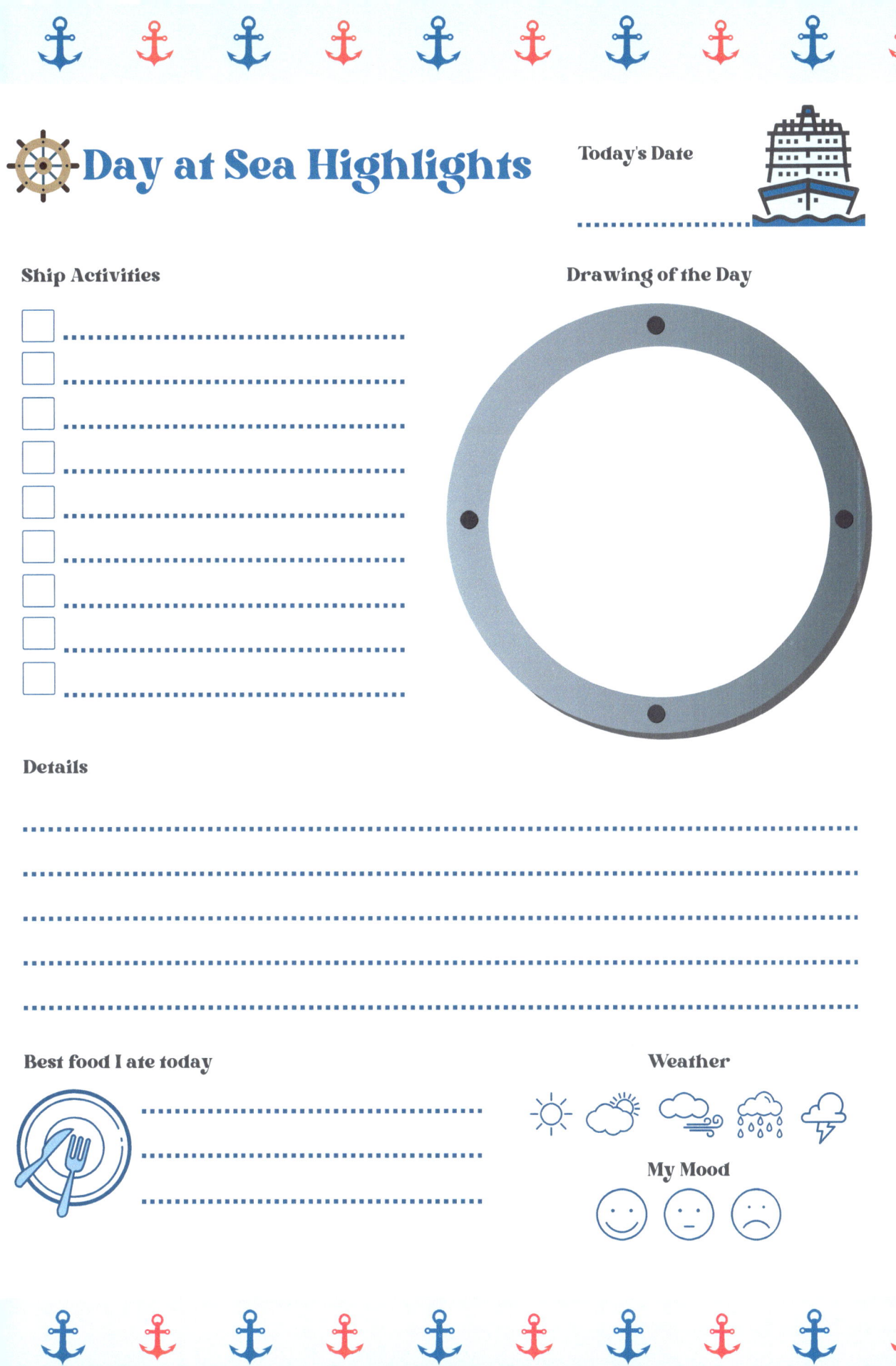

Port Day Highlights

Today's Date

....

Port Activities

....
....
....
....
....

Something Special about Today

....
....
....
....
....

Details

....
....
....
....
....
....
....
....
....
....
....
....
....

Weather

My Mood

Day at Sea Highlights

Today's Date
....

Ship Activities

- ☐ ....
- ☐ ....
- ☐ ....
- ☐ ....
- ☐ ....
- ☐ ....
- ☐ ....
- ☐ ....
- ☐ ....

Drawing of the Day

Details

....
....
....
....
....

Best food I ate today

....
....
....

Weather

My Mood

Port Day Highlights

Today's Date

....

Port Activities

....
....
....
....
....

Something Special about Today

....
....
....
....
....

Details

....
....
....
....
....
....
....
....
....
....
....
....
....

Weather

My Mood

Pirate Night - Aaargh!

Today's Date

....

Ship Activities

....
....
....
....

Me as a Pirate

Favorite thing I ate

....
....
....

What I did

....
....
....
....

My favorite part

....
....
....
....

Day at Sea Highlights

Today's Date

....

Ship Activities

- [ ] ....
- [ ] ....
- [ ] ....
- [ ] ....
- [ ] ....
- [ ] ....
- [ ] ....
- [ ] ....
- [ ] ....

Drawing of the Day

Details

....
....
....
....
....

Best food I ate today

....
....
....

Weather

My Mood

Disembarkation Day

Today's Date

....

My last meal on the ship

....
....
....

What I liked most about this ship

....
....
....
....

Going Home: How are we getting there? How long will it take?

....
....
....
....

At home, I am most looking forward to:

....
....
....
....

Things to Remember

A friend I made

Something I tried to do

Favorite food I ate

Favorite port of call

Something funny that happened

Something new I learned

The best part of the trip

A souvenir I got

Looking Back

I will always remember when

....
....
....
....
....

What do I most want to remember about this trip?

Favorite Photos

Favorite Photos

Treasure Hunt Maze

Which way leads to the treasure island?

Connect The Dots

Connect the dots and color in the hidden picture.

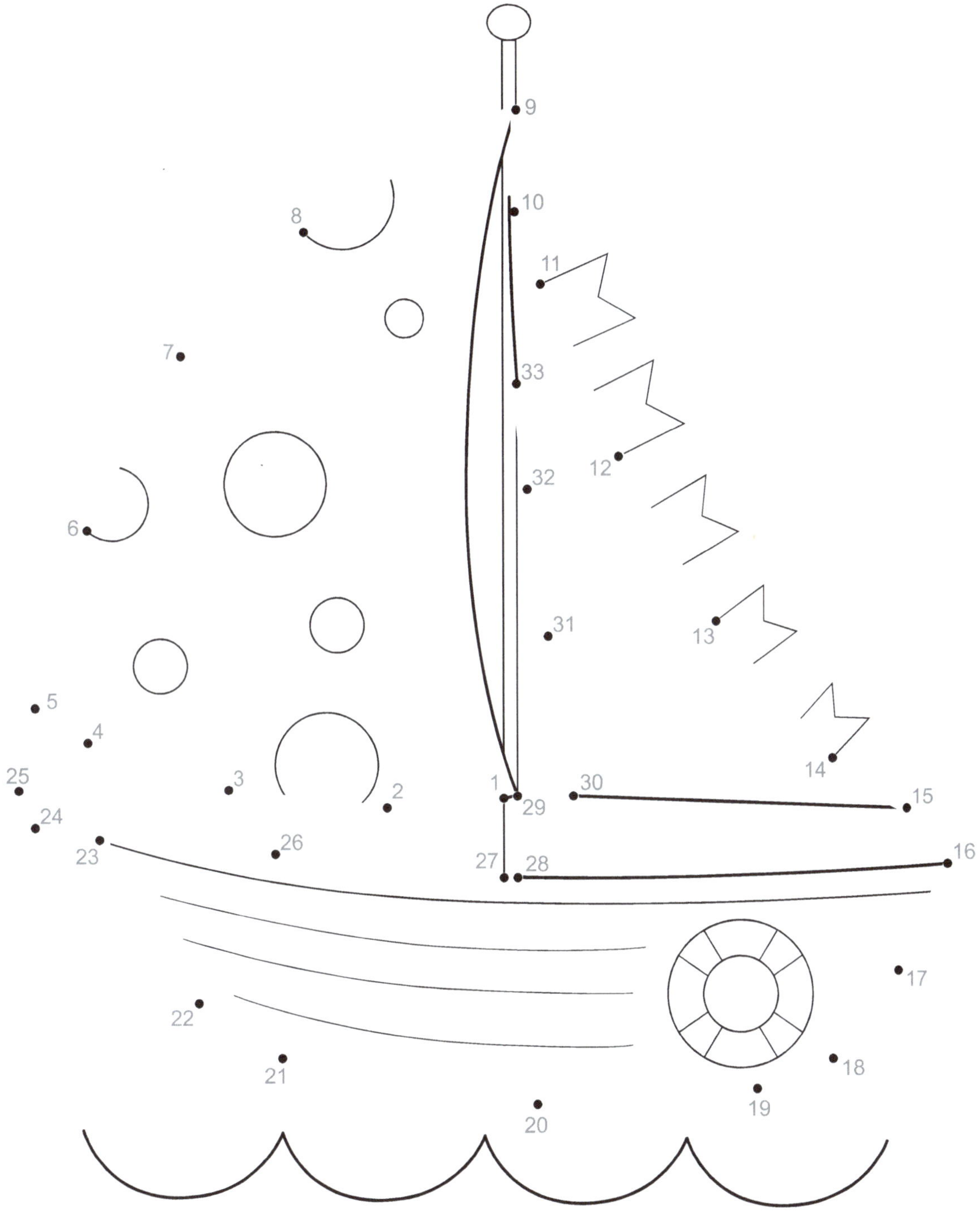

Word Search

Can you find the words hidden in the puzzle?

```
S A I L M M Y L C E M T
L H S N R O A H O T U R
T E L E S C O P E R S E
O T A L C W I I D Y I A
F E N C C N Y R B O O S
L R D C O M P A S S H U
A S S O R O R T A F E R
G T T S L S U E N Y I E
G O W L C O I N S R L O
O D R M I N Y D S H I P
L M H A R P E N N N S D
D C A P T A I N R E G Y
```

CAPTAIN	ISLAND	GOLD
TREASURE	TELESCOPE	FLAG
MAP	PIRATE	COINS
SAIL	COMPASS	SHIP

Drawing Activity

Draw the outside view on cruise ship.

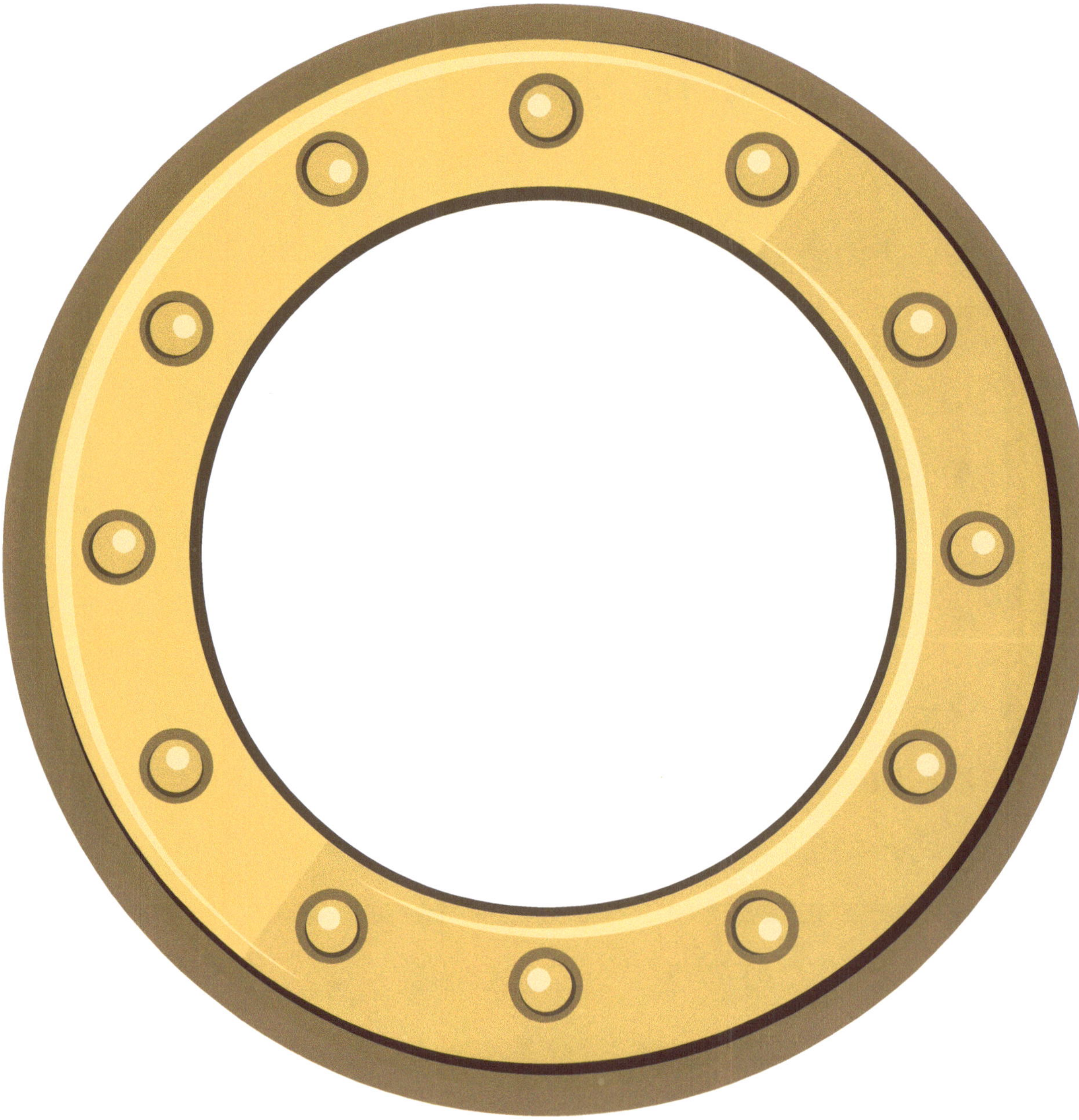

Drawing Activity

Draw the other side to finish the picture.

⚓ Tic Tac Toe Chart

Players take turns placing one chip until a player has 3 in a row. Horizontal, vertical, and diagonal are each valid winning rows.

Copyright© 2022 by Bookfly Publishing

No part of this publication may be reproduced, stored in a retrieval system, or transmitted in any form or by any means, electronic, mechanical, photocopying, recording, or otherwise, without the written permission of the publisher. Limited Liability/Disclaimer of Warranty. The publisher and the author make no representation or warranties with the respect to the accuracy or completeness of the contents of this work and specifically disclaim all warranties including without limitation warranties for a particular purpose. No warranty may be created or extended by sales or promotional materials. The advice or strategies contained herein may not be suitable for every situation. This work is sold with the understanding that the publisher is not engaged in rendering medical, legal, or other professional advice or services. Neither the publisher nor the author or creator shall be liable for damages arising.

For general information on our other products and services please visit www.bookflypublishing.com or contact us at info@bookflypublishing.com.
Bookfly Publishing publishes its books and materials in a variety of electronic and print formats. Some content that appears in print may not be available in electronic books and vice versa.

ISBN 978-1-7369393-8-3
All rights reserved. Published by Bookfly Publishing
Harvey, Louisiana
www.bookflypublishing.com

Printed in the USA

www.ingramcontent.com/pod-product-compliance
Lightning Source LLC
Chambersburg PA
CBHW050747110526
44590CB00003B/101